Lorien House, publisher
P.O. Box 1112
Black Mountain, North Carolina
28711

FIRST EDITION   June 1980

ISBN 0-934852-21-9

CASTLES & CLOUDS

CASTLES & CLOUDS - Prologue

We dream castles constructed of clouds, battlements
of ice-palace frivolity, rising to confront our
sensibility. We dream drawbridge access to the
fantasy of our souls, the wondrous worlds woven in
memory of time gone by. We dream ...

... And in our dream we reach beyond the mundane
limitations of our selves, and reach into the
reality beyond our concrete world. We hope, and
in our hope we build castles for our delight. We
construct mist enshrouded shrines to our constant
struggle for greater plateaus of accomplishment.

We are surrounded by childhood hauntings reaching
through lost time, and bridging the moat of our
present despair. The past reverberates through-
out the present reality of our lives to bring forth
a new understanding. Our misconceptions are molded
into new patterns of truth, and we gain entry to
our dreamworld castles.

Clouds evolve from the constructs of our minds,
mushrooming into being, flowing in constant flux,
forming exotic shapes, crowding the horizon with
multitudinous menageries. There are suggestions
of men, quick of foot or bestial in lazing forms,
changing into hideous beasts of prey. Castles and
dragons ... one evolving into the construct of the
other, exchanging roles in the ever progressing
reality of clouds.

Castles and Clouds: They are but facets of each
other, mirrors of their own reality, evolving one
into the other endlessly, silently. They beckon
to us to cross our many ages of miscomprehension
to find new answers in a final gateway of the
mind.

*

Soft was her touch,
Tender the dream.
She gazed once more
From memory's stream.

CLOUD EPISODES

I.

I see lightening singing sweet songs
Over valley depths. One belongs
Perched upon scenic hills watching
Cloud episodes passing, catching
Upon occasional mountain
Peaks, spewing into dells to gain
The farther side. One needs to see
Stories written, yet flowing free.

II.

The gathering storm threatens me
Only distantly - for I see
The grandeur of the cloud-filled sky,
The beauty ... without knowing why
Panoramas of change were wrought
By an unseen hand. I once thought
Clouds formed a land free of time's hand
And longed to walk the sky-bound strand.

III.

Strange alabaster forms mount tall,
Ranging upward in pillars; all
Sculpted by wind-blown artisans
Into that of a famous man's
Face or torso to inspire each
Who witness the event to teach
Others to see the artist's whim
In creating vistas for him.

IV.

Even the storm-driven clouds bear
Lines of grace and hurry to share
The dreams of sunny days yet to be -
Sky songs just for you and for me.
Sometimes I sit and I ponder
Cumulous wonders that wander
Across vast prairies of blue sea,
Seeming lost, yet wondrously free.

V.

Thoughts race over my sky of mind
And yet somehow I always find
Room to halt - for a time - and know
The valley shade in summer's glow.
Whether clouds of storm, or feather
Caress, I learn daily weather
Brings scenic changes to my view -
Yet always reminds me of you.

VI.

If memories were clouds, you would
See why you and I never could
Cling to the realms of yesterday.
Time rules life in every way
With no concern for what has passed.
It is whisked away, changed at last
Into new imaginations
Of evolving cloud creations.

VII.

And I watch cloud episodes play
Before my eyes every day
Knowing each sculpture shown to me
Has not been seen before; yet surely
Composed of myriad fragments
Collected from scattered events
Of my lingering thoughts of you -
A tale etched on my mind in blue.

***

Cloud beast forms surge from behind mountain
ridges, seething skyward in tumbling profusion.
Rank upon rank they march eastward, seeking
distant realms unknown to those bound to the earth.
Ceaseless they continue, the evening sun
shimmering on their out-thrust shoulders, their
stalwart backs.

And occasionally a distant flash of lightening,
a burst of crackling discharge, connects us but
momentarily to the new unexplored world of Cloud.
Something stirs deep within, a vague longing to
tread vast leagues of the irregular cotton surface,

to climb evolving Everests in an attempt to reach
their Himalyan summits, towering above all that is
known and witnessed by man - realm of the eagles,
palacial sky wealth of beauty.

Someday ... someday I will walk the winding paths
of Cloud, lost in the wonder world of new
continuous creation. Someday I will find the new
adventure I seek beyond the known.

*

ON CLOUDS ...
                    Waiting valley,
            Deeper than the many
            And varied valleys of Earth,
            How you call to me
            To walk
            Your soft cushioned path.
                    You descend
            Through intricate whorls
            Feathery features,
            Crystal creations swirling
            In everchanging,
            Rearranging patterns.
                    So deep your valley
            That the sun never brightens
            The untrodden floor
            And I wonder evermore
            If a chance shall come
            When I may find the way.
                    Ice crystal fringes
            Alit with sun glimmer
            Brightness,
            A golden highlight
            Tracing myriad branchings

Of your mysterious maze.
        And you are so delicate
In your carefree days,
Coursing across the cold
Featureless plain of sky
Hurrying to realms
Unknown to me.

*

The sky stood forth today,
      blue immensity
      filling even the distant corners
            of my mind.
Crystal clarity, even the air
      seemed pure - rare ether.
And clouds - what enormous
      beasts reared from
      fast mountain fortresses,
                        challenging -
      always vying for
                  far horizons ...
White fomenting evolutions
      pushed their way
      across silken skies,
Castle fortresses surging
      forward
      to the land of tomorrow ...

*

Seeking valley windings of clouded topographies,
rivers of sun slip over the wind sculpted edge
and pour in waterfalls of beams to the waiting
earth.

They splash in torrents of radiance, spilling into
pools of summer. Sparkling columns of light
cascade onto fields of green, bathing them with
the freshness of life.

*

Range upon range
Mountainous wonder
Fading image repetitions
Into distant horizons of blue -
Sky-cloud projection
Slipping across Blue Ridge patterns
Sending quick shadows
Dancing into distant memories -
Sun-patch irregularities
Bursting upon wood and meadow
Spotlight shadowshow
Green tone optic shifts -
Summer days again
Soon to pass   Gone too quick
For proper thought
And gentle rest.

*

THE MIDNIGHT STORM

It raced before the wind,
Sailing the uncharted sky
Giving threat to harbors
In the night - warm home fires
Burning low. Dark clouds poured
Into waiting valleys,
Erasing the moonlight
And distant stars. It walked
Across the floor of the
Silent waiting valley
On stilted feet of fire,
Heavy flashing tread of
The wind-borne gods - night omens.

All hope vanished from the
Might of the midnight storm.

*

The morning was sunless with an opaque fog
floating through the cool damp air in purposeless
motion. He awoke to find a room, strange with
ornate surroundings reflecting expensive tastes
not his own.

He lay still, waiting for the final moment of this
interim of wake-sleeping when he would know his
familiar drab morning-lit room in his home.

Every glance brought forth his new surroundings,
real yet not within his memory. He dressed,
roamed through halls and down the winding
staircase of marble, cold to the touch, and into
the room with the crackling warm fire created by

apparently no one, waiting for appreciation.

Escape registered on his mind, a recognition need pressing in from unthought corners. He opened the main door and stepped into fog, thick cream in the damp morning.

The columns rose to the portico embracing space in ancient perfection of man's wisdom preserved from the acid, time. He stepped out, finding steps fading down into fog; marble steps worn deep by feet rising from the unseen plains and descending to the same through morning fog, damp and cold.

He descended carefully to the bottom step before the ground, covered artfully by the mist. Fear sense told him to stop and measure how far to the bottom. He reached, but felt not; looked, but saw not.

The building so tall and majestic rested with comfort on groundless fog in the unknown earth sky. He turned and re-entered, knowing to wake again soon in the drab bed he knew all too well, feeling hard ground where soft tread step should be.

*

Father of storms, Old Man of Cloud,
Frowning down onto rain-soaked earth,
Craggy features, flowing beard sweeping
Across wide valleys of green;
Flanked by towering cloud forms,
The Pillars of Shakka.

*

Naked walks the day
Through fields of summer
Storm, tempestuous
Childhood memory.

Silence comes to play
Bringing light motifs
To mind upon winds
Of calm harmony.

If but a fleeting
Thought, a play on time
Lost to all but thee,
Yet may I find youth.

Ideas I send winging,
Messengers of speed
Crossing unknown lengths
Of life to bring truth.

And truth yet shall stand
Naked as the dawn:
Light to waiting land
Where new life shall spawn.

*

MOUNTAIN MEMORY

I.

From the sun calmed alluvial plain
It rose, first but a gentle flaw
Upon the maiden's cheek - a strain
Hidden among the forests tall.
In death-throe agony the ground
Heaved, rumbling forth discontented,
Lifting blocks of granite. A sound
Boomed through the air, earth wrath vented.

II.

Fingers of stone now reached upward
Seeking the sun, rising as one
Continent of anger. Rocks poured
Down the new-created slopes, a run
Onto once peaceful fields of grass,
Covering once-known ways of life.
A mountain reality, rock mass
Sermon - bringing new days of strife.

III.

Rising to the sky, volcanoes
Gushing ash, belching smoke and fires
In violent expression - earth woes.
Lava poured around mountain spires
Easing onto the waiting plain.
The earth quaked, tossed in unpent ire
Upon its bottomlands the rain
Of granite. And rose yet higher.

IV.

Time brought peace and stability
To the scene of former violence,
Bringing wind and rain to gently
Sculpt the crude blocks with due patience.
Ages passed with second-hand ease
To a later era where man
Awoke to greet the dawn, and trees
Strove to cross where the mountains stand.

V.

Now the tranquil time-worn mountain
Ranges bring to mind thoughts of peace.
Cloud shadows cross the valley plain
Then climb forest carpets of trees
With heavenly ease; sun deprived
Acres stretch beyond the limits
Of mind or eye. A sudden drive
By sunbeam light, and darkness quits.

VI.

Gone forever are the old days
When giants crossed these ancient peaks
In but a few strides. Gone their ways
Are these singular beings, strange freaks
In our minds - yet of man a race
Once in abundance. Now they've gone -
Erased without leaving a trace,
Known to us now in tales alone.

VII.

Gone also are the woodland sprites,
Nymphs and dryads of yesteryear,
Dwellers of forest and field. Nights
Find empty trees alone and drear.
And gone are flitting silver wings,
Faint tinkling on the wind. A mood
Felt by the inhabitants brings
Memories of such to the wood.

VIII.

Once sun-filtered forests stood tall
In a collective confidence -
A promise remembered by all
Of protection and growth from whence
All life does flow. But time brought change
On winds of chance, and time did freeze
The glory of the forest range
And slowly the sprites left their trees.

IX.

A touch of magic, extra light
Among the many tints of green
Faded from existence, but might
Perhaps be found if you but dream
While walking with soft winding tread.
You may see a hint of this glow
By being woven in the thread
Of timeless trails.   You then shall know.

X.

A forest yet alive with spirit
Continuity is rare, one
Of few of ancient stock. To sit
In such a place finds time undone
But momentarily, and you
Are in forest then as if now,
Spanning a universe seen true
To witness the essence of flow.

XI.

Although you may not find hidden
Groves of magic and beauty,
Enjoy the day in grassy glen
Watching tumbling brooks dance so free
Over waiting rocks to now race
To further depths, then resting fair
In sudden becalmed pools. No trace
Of excitement is mirrored there.

XII.

Reflective pools lend thought to you
Recalled in your splashing brilliance.
Ripple patterns give a fresh view
To mountain reality, a trance
Weaving secret silver stories
Into my mind as I linger
At the edge of the stream; for these
Tapestries let memories stir.

XIII.

Between mountain crests, by countless
Rivulets fed, flows the wide stream -
Valley pride. A waterfall tress
Feeds this river, and it may seem
Enchanted in its gentle fall
From rocky overhead so sheer;
Streamers cascading, splashing, call
Musical tones to waiting ear.

XIV.

The river snakes, weaves, curls and winds
Itself around the foothill slopes
Relentlessly until it finds
The alluvial plain. One hopes
The restless river brings good news
Of natural wonders waiting
Beyond our crowded avenues
For us to share, our quest sating.

XV.

One hopes the distant mountain range
Caught in a sunset purple haze
Will remain to us new and strange,
A paradise to explore. Days
May pass and find us adventure
Bound to wilderness mountain ground.
And ways may pass, our footing sure
Upon endless trails, safe and sound.

XVI.

Our mountain memory, it feeds
Later days with occasional
Tales of summer trails. It but needs
A careless hint and we recall
Our days of youth and enchantment
When first we experienced this
Land of wooded giants and spent
Our fleeting hours in sunlit bliss.

***

I would have liked to talk with Robert Frost,
Or with Shelley share a rhyme or two.
To hear Will Shakespeare weave his verbal nets
Of love with which to encapture my soul;
To but see the poets ancient, creators
Of many a verse, would lift my lone heart
To higher realms of thought and happiness.
But to this fine goal I cannot climb
For alas, I am of another time.

*

Life is a palace of pleasant surprises, a mansion
of memorable moments stored almost regretfully in
the many rooms of the past until at last we sleep
for a time - only to awaken once more in a house
new and not familiar to us with echoing carpetless
corridors, unlit stairways and a countless
abundance of empty rooms, as if waiting for the
dawn and life to fill once more each corner with
thoughts of joy, whisperings from sunlit days and
children's ways as we again wander our palacial
wildernesses seeking, it seems, a place to rest
and another night of dreams.

*

As the sun boils over morning mountains, so I
drive my chariot of life beyond known realms of
being. As fierce rays of light temper patient
earth, so too I wage my days in earnest quest of
better ways. I wait not for chance, opportunist
it may be, but wade into golden-hued reality
streams seeking fleeting dreams of ever coming
tomorrows. Reflections cast clarity conceptions
into my roiling mind, bring thoughts kind and
serene to the ethereal surface of that endless
sea of self.

*

He shook his head, long white hair lifting, falling
in waves, wild yet orderly in a rhythm of muscular
movement. His eyes glistened, a sparkle of
enchantment thrown out upon the shadows of night.
The horse stood proud, erect in his beauty, alert
to every sound.

I watched, motionless in anticipation: Would I be
able to capture him? His stance was postured for
flight if necessary, but he clung to the moment,
willing to stay in all his splendor until danger
presented itself. The muscles of his neck and
flanks rippled with the excitement of fear, of not
knowing.

Poised in the moonlight, steam flared from his
nostrils, breath of fire, strength embodied in the
night. He pawed the ground lightly, quietly,
listening for a sound. So beautiful he was, I was
reluctant to give chase, for I knew once tamed he
would never be the same. The flavor of freedom
would be sapped. He would be mine then, a strong
brilliant creature of the wilds broken by a man.
Only necessity drove me on.

I stepped from cover and cast my lariat. It sailed
through the air, silently falling short of the
stallion's head. I knew my reluctance would free
him. He bolted in a burst of strength, a fury cast
into the night. He galloped away, a dwindling
night creature under the light of the silvered
moon, a wraith of the shadows, flitting through
trees, now across an open field.

I watched, knowing there would be another time
when I would find this mysterious animal, and
perhaps then I would not be so reluctant.

*

Many sounds came to my hearing. Occasional
innocent mooing of the cows of the field drifted
up to me. I could pinpoint the many pastures and
see the small brown forms dotting the landscape.
The sound of a chainsaw starting up, changing in
crescendo as it attacked a tree ... The sound was
harsh on the landscape, loud and hard to locate.
A shudder of leaves in the wood to my left ... a
popping sound ... then the fatal crashing of a
toppled monarch. A gap appeared in the trees,
tops waving, a few leaves floating on the air, and
a transparent wall of light brown dust filtered
through the trees.

I stood for what may have been a long while,
absorbing all sounds and smells, taking them into
myself. I rejoiced within for the beauty
surrounding me in this unknown place yet to be
discovered by the people crowding other trails of
the Summer.

I exhaled a gentle sigh, then chose my step for
continuing along this singular path wending through
the days.

*

There is something about mountains that is
beautiful and inspiring. Perhaps it is simply the
ability to gaze vast distances and ponder
mysterious hidden valleys or ribbon roads that
thread their way to the sun. Perhaps it is a
feeling of appreciation for their size after
toiling upward for half an hour.

*

MY MUSE

I shall remember elysium days
When we strolled uncharted ways
In contentment. And I shall recall
Star sprinkled nights when life had hope.

And now? Where has love gone;
Filtering through grasping need,
Pouring in streams of regret.
Where is this phantom Life
Slipping to in sly stealth?

Perhaps it shall again return
With as silent a tread as it left;
Perhaps I shall awaken
To that familiar call of life
And know you return to me
Hidden behind yet another disguise.

I almost remember times
Between time when you review
Your many wiles, faces, smiles
Which you shall try on me once more
As we play our well-rehearsed parts.

I shall look for elysium days
When we shall find limitless ways
To recall this our eternal game.
Come, my Muse, and erase my frown.

*

Old railroad stations, abandoned to time's
unrelenting erosion - peeling paint, window broken
dust laden relics of busy years - signs creaking
in early morning winds. Large wheel baggage carts
waiting, rails rusting in the tender dawn light,
distant trainwail warnings, track hum vibration ...

... then a singular cyclopean light hanging in the
distance, light reflecting on travel-polished
rails, racing forward as the train finally arrives,
growing from a minute being into gargantuan steel
proportions ...

... The train and its cars, old dirt-laden paint,
dark with age, seats faded and threadbare in
places, echoing from an affluent era, forgotten
now in highway rush. Central city railway stations
all but abandoned, footsteps echoing on tile
labyrinths to nowhere, side passages boarded up,
offices closed forever, waiting patiently for a
rebirth not about to take place ...

... Old men doing old jobs, train, conductor and
engineer, fading alike into the forgetful past,
gold watch punctuality lost to bygone days ...
Time has proven once more that The Twentieth
Century, Limited is just that ...

*

Stones ... not worn by the feet of the
multitudes, but pock-marked by abuse.

*

I want to be able to walk in spring woods, to
breathe the freshness of unknown air.

Earn, says a voice.

I want to watch autumn leaves silently drift to
the awaiting stretches of grass, disturbed only
by the rude poking of hungry squirrels.

Work, demands the world.

Without the warmth of the daily sun, without the
sparkle of unwatched streams, without the radiant
joy of vast grasslands, I feel torn, destroyed in
the youth of my life as an unfortunate sapling.

Slave, is the command.

I need to be able to sit, and think. I need to
be able to escape from the hateful and uncaring
world into which we are all thrown.

Pay, they warn.

*

I have found in the endless intertwinings of my
soul a nexus to oblivion, a path to the glory of
universal discontinuity. I have found in my
lifetime wanderings a thread of continuation woven
into patternless pi calculations. I have sought
and found nothingness in the everywhere of the
world, have floated in pools of dejection with
mindless thoughts emptying out onto plains of
misunderstanding as flood overflows cast them-
selves into valley realities heedless of the
consequences.

*

All the measured heartbeats, all the remembered
pains - life in a breath. Reality but a simple
thought, an imagined sequence, coming, going. It
fades with morning light, withers under the heat
of day.

A voice cries "Wake! End this crazy dream, this
absurd enchantment." My body quivers a response,
acknowledges its unreality, fears its dissolvement.
A lifetime, a dream. Wake, and a soul dies,
floats through the window in time, rises, and is
lost.

Stay another moment, breathe one more time.
Continue this play - a sham with five full acts,
interwoven with myriad scenes of lengthy pains,
fleeting joys.

I walk down the street, the wind pushing me back,
forcing a walk forward in retrospect. The trees,
winter-death apparent, sway in turmoil, reach for
me, to pluck me skyward, lift me into the black
night, lost in the terrible scream of naked
starlight.

On my right houses are sheltered against life,
enclosing each upon its own artificial warmth,
devoid of time and happiness.

On my left, a small dead tree, on its side, a
crucified Christmas tree bleeding strands of
tinfoil, forlorn, symbolizing something apparent,
yet totally alien to my conscious, screaming its
message in another tongue, sweet babble to my ears.

Wake! cries a voice deep within its secluded skull.
Wake to warmth, comfort. Let the cold, senseless
frame, shadow of reality die where it stands.
What use is it, blundering through moonless night,
gathering harvests of ample pain, grasping at

self-entertainment with cold numb fingers, losing
grip, falling through seven eternities of failure,
tumbling headlong through vacant hollow corridors
toward a far miniature door forever closed, never
reaching even the ultimate failure - failing at
being a failure, succeeding only once, reaching a
nothingness while being surrounded by mocking
torments from the frail past.

Footsteps echo on cold dead streets moonlit in
darkness. Footsteps approach, pass, disappear
into a wall of night as each walks his own empty
small corridor to nothing, from nothing -
accomplishing nothing.

*

Listen not to the noises of the night;
They sing to you lyrics of solitude.
Heed not the murmurs as night wings take flight,
Lest you find creatures of the dark intrude
        upon your mind
                quaking heart
                        to find
        dim corridors
                empty
                        and hollow
                of hope
                in the night
        and fright
                clinging
                        to your mind.
Listen not to the noises of the night,
 Chirrups and wailing cries deep in the gloom;
Listen not to banshee screams far from your sight.
 Do not kindle dread, sitting in your room;

                    but sleep
                              in peace
          for your fears
                              are unfounded -
          lonely thoughts
          upon fields of apprehension.
     Smile
               when deep in your world
                              of sleep.
               Think of sunlit trails,
          paths slipping across
               fields of emerald
                              and
     Listen not to the noises of the night.

                         *

Sunlight dappled leaf patterns floating in pools
of shade sheltered forest, cool meandering brook
breaking forth into field freshness, dancing on
rock-stage performances; sun mirror diamond facet
water flow, flashing, splashing gem brilliance
ripple pattern rapids slipping around granite
steadfastness, adamantine solidarity. Time guides
myriad stream patterns across field expanse,
weaving snake trail differentiations, rope-trick
eon realities, too subtle for thought or exper-
ience. Mountain stability eternity, flowing hills
of carpet greenery, rock outcrops showing craggy
faces to the sky - wait patiently for man's
passing, old scars knitting under sun tender
touch, healing beams of light slipping between
cloud clusters to caress careless quiet structure
conceptualizations of earth reality. So short,
so quickly passes the experience named man; so
slight influence is made in total time erased
memory of lingering traces of his attempt to

create lasting monuments to eternity. Lost in
time are feeble memorabilia buried within sedimen-
tary graves, fossil fuels for future generations.

*

Autumn ... and night-filled roads slip through
silent waiting hills. A distant dog
barks his suspicion, rousing another
one further along the road. Silent
cool mists hang in the valley,
filtering the timeless night air as
I walk midnight mountain roads,
moonless travels to morning
destinations.

*

Autumn, when leaves fall helplessly
At the mercy of the cold wind.
Autumn, when trees admit secrets
Of color-laden consciousness
Hidden throughout the summer fair.
Yes, O Autumn, you speak of death
With beauty on your painted tongue.
You show us life in its decline,
Yet you bear the fruit and the seed
Of a new life; of a new hope
To yet be seen when the winter
Snows are but faded memories
In sun-warmed hearts.

*

THE WIND

The wind, fleeting lover
Of earthbound ways,
Rakes its fingers
Through the leaf-hair
Of waiting trees.
Gentle wind, combing
Caresses into forests
Of contentment,
Bring your hushed
Sighs to me ...
Sing your ballad
To my listening
Self ...
                    And dance,
O wind, with me.
Twirl me in roundelays
Of morning song,
Beat three-quarter time
In natural waltzes
Of summer days
                          free
From the press
Of hot, cloudless
Ways of men.

Remember, O wind,
Times long passed
When you in your youth
Flowed ever on,
Tendrils

Of scented air
Carrying life
To new-born continents
Of experience.
And remember times
When rage whelmed
Within
And you spewed
Destruction
Upon the earth,
Etching whirling doom
Upon nature's breast.

O wind,
How terrible you were ...
And yet ... even then
Deep within
Your vented anger
Dwelled
Your gentler side
Willing to hide
Until a better day
When quiet forests
Would beg audience
To your sweet performance.
        Dance yet once more
With me
O wind. Send me
                    spinning
Across sleepy glades
With the joy
Of your song.
Swirl your delight
Upon autumnal
Forest floors,
Spright leafy pavanes
Performed for me,
                    O wind.

*

I choose the wind, the early morning sun on a
mist-veiled mountain side. I choose the free roar
of the cold, yet inviting ocean. I choose the
pine-scented forest, the rose-fragrance of a warm
southern summer breeze, the soft and light bubbling
of a new-born brook dancing over the rough terrain
in search of some still, secluded pool.

*

Back ... behind the hissing of the night wind -
a deeper sound, a dull muffled roar,
timeless wind-call, shifting of eternal
sands, sum of storm-bred power ...
moving measureless air currents age-old
memories stirred, torn loose from
foundations of daylight clarity -
bringing ancient thoughts, haunting
dreams down corridors of night, galactic
winds whistling mountain fastness, ocean
fluidity, star hope among strains of
dark despair, end-world concepts, subtle
fears filtering into consciousness
during brief moments of soft reflection ......

*

Sorrow is like a plant ... water it and it will
grow - starve it and it will die.

Joy is like a plant ...

*

Summer, and the morning sun is caught in staid
high-rise apartment windows: myriad reflections
multiple suns golden burning heavenly fires in the
misted dawn.

Summer, and gentle winds stir fields of ripening
wheat shudder wave undulations coursing across
golden grains in afternoon sun.

Summer, and heat weaves into distant realities
distorting warping caressing sight strain
panoramas.

Summer, and people are driven to scorching sands
in senseless hordes crowding once lonely
beachheads in fleshy abundance.

Summer, and I find my feet wandering distant
roads of the mind, empty highways of night
memory, seeking new-found fields of contentment
with paved persistence.

Summer, and time eases toward autumn - sly
silent autumn, slipping into awareness through
careless unhinged doors of sunlit green warmth
to haunt taunt with cold draft persistence
until one finally closes the door.

*

Words - they are but fragments, cells of my
living self frozen in time.

*

The river arches its sinuous back over moss car-
peted rocks, spilling beyond, into waiting pools
of crystalline purity. The strong current ripples
the surface in a band of refracted light; pebbly
bottoms warp continuously. Side-waters are still,
cloud-form reflections showing immense depth in
sky blue scenarios ... seemingly great depth both
above and below. We are but frail creatures
caught between infinities.

Mist hangs above the water where it weaves between
steep hills, under spreading oak and elm, into
vales of continuous shade ... mist hangs above
the water and creates a world separate from normal
sun-filled days. The river course becomes a
reality apart from others - a myth in the minds of
men, recalling age-lost times, ancestral memory,
where life was an awesome furtiveness and valleys
of shade protected unknown beings ...

Occasionally the sun filters through the leaf
canopy, penetrating the river floor in surprising
momentary shafts of light, creating silver sparkle
flash fire wavering ... then gone. Sunlight-
shadowshow play inspires images of strange beast
forms slipping through shrub cover, waiting ...
waiting for hapless wanderers in supernal glens
of day.

Yet beauty mixes with awe but seldom. The forest
of day and river of slender continuity do not
normally spark realms of imagination. Not often
does the song of mystic worlds come flowing into
the life of man. The golden harp strums softly
in the recesses of memory, haunting slumbering
minds with the magic of greater worlds than the
only one we know ...

*

She came out of my reverie, a ghost out of future
thoughts, yet real, striding concrete walks with
assurance. Then she passed, fading into the dim
horizons of memory.

*

We came to a gateway, and on the other side was a
fantastic world of material, an Expo '79. We
paid our money, took our ticket, and entered
through the gateway.

The world of material was so absorbing that we
forgot how we entered, forgot where the gate was
located - forgot even that a gate existed. We
enjoyed all the beautiful and subtle entrapments
for a long time, until one day it dawned on us
that there was a gateway, and that we had entered
this fantastic plastic pleasure palace from some-
place else, someplace forgotten in time and in
experience.

Our carny life suddenly went sour, and we wandered
unmapped ways, seeking the gateway memory within
ourselves. One hope, one encouragement was that
one of our friends made it, found the mythical
gateway. Having found the way free, he waits,
encouraging us, trying to help us back home.

The catch to our venture is that we cannot let
this material world sour on us, we cannot let it
weight us down. We must work to make this world
understood and beautiful, work to make ourselves
free of its many entrapments. Then the gateway
shall appear everywhere, surrounding us in our
newfound freedom of consciousness.

*

If you had a puzzle before you, almost assembled,
lacking only a few pieces - and if you had those
pieces in your hand ... would you walk away and
finish it tomorrow, or would you do it today?

*

Fireflies are lifting from the night-enshrouded
ground ... fiery sparks gently arcing skyward ...
golden orbs of pale light against a backdrop of
dusk-hue green ... fairy lamps dancing across
quiet fields and through quickly darkening wooded
hills, following trails marked only in the
imagination ... above, lamps floating amongst the
dark and still leaves of the Mallorn trees ...
and we rest our horses in the gathering dusk,
seeking a campsite near the never-ending stone
paved road of our destiny ...

*

I know now why people spoke of seeing fairies
dancing in the wood, or elves on a march. I saw
them passing, holding aloft their firefly lanterns,
slipping through the trees. Dryads and hamadryads
twinkled from their perches, witnessing the silent
procession. Occasionally the lanterns would
vanish, as if frightened by some noise; then would
relight further along the trail.

*

We find ourselves caught in the sparkling web of
the eternal Now, our commitment enmeshed by acts
within the realms of time.

Yet we bask in the ever promising Not Now, com-
prised of the committed Past of life, the Future
of multiple possibilities, the unenacted Present
... we lounge in forever imaginings of that which
is not.

We experience the interstices of Now and Not Now,
the eternally interwoven warp and woof of soul
reality. We experience interaction momentarily,
aware of our positions upon this rock-strewn
planet Earth.

*

The solar eclipse ... a small group gathered on a
knoll in the Spring woods ... gentle insect and
bird songs filtering into our consciousnesses ...

Time evolves slowly and an arc of darkness eases
itself across the fiery disk of sun. Shadows
slip through the forest, quieting all sounds,
absorbing the light innuendoes of the wooded land.
The last second of light is a spark of brilliance
from the sun's very edge, a gem in the sky of
sudden night, slender beams of momentray light
flashing, then gone.

Darkness rules all, silence - a hush of tremendous
depth hugs the beings of the forest, urges utter
quiet as time passes. Cold sunless winds stir
the leaves and branches ... a cold never warmed
by our fiery lord, blowing, ever blowing in the
shadow of the sun, racing across the earth in the
path of the eclipse, seeking the shadowed lands.

Time having traced its appointed route, a sliver
of light appears, heralding the return of the
sun's light and of life itself. The forest goes
from night dark to a fragile silver, every leaf,
every bough transformed to a precious metal,
glistening; the silver evolves into gold, the soft
darker burnishing of pure gold; the gold then
becomes a soft Spring green, then a darker green,
then the various colorations of the forest in its
natural state. A bird gives a questionning
chirrup, then breaks forth with its song, the
wakening of morning after such a short night.

The shadow is gone, the sun shines in all its
glory - yet all warmth is gone. Cold winds buffet
us and urge our seeking further sun safe from
the breezes of the wintry North.

*

CASTLES AND CLOUDS - Epilogue

We dream clouds interweaving anthropomorphic
shapes into the seeming reality of our lives.
We dream clouds in wondrous shapes and hues
becoming symbolic expressions of our deepest
desires ... and we dream life as we would wish
it to progress, tasting the pleasures of serenity
and happiness, free from the maddened chaos we
find surrounding us.

As clouds form only to dissolve into other shapes,
so we too evolve from our sheltered youth into
wizened creatures, tattered on the rocks of
experience, buffeted by the many winds of chance.
And where can we turn, once we are diminished by
the storms of life?

In our youth, we were gods upon the Earth, tasting
its many gifts, revelling in the sunshine of its
many days, endless for us in those days of
innocence. We were gods, rightful heirs to our
kingdom stretched out before us. And when did
we fall? When did we corrupt our godhood if not
upon maturity to the ways of man on Earth.
Innocence guided us around the innumerable pit-
falls of life's rewards. We yet seek for a time
of innocence, never more that a grasp away, yet
always beyond our limited sight.

We build castles of regret from the clouds of our
accomplishments, admiring our constructs, but not
admitting the uselessness of the project before
us. It is not the reality which we desire, and
falls far short of our expectations.

We must turn now from our limited artistries and
seek anew the age of innocence we once knew. We
must cease striving in mazes of misunderstanding
and begin to re-create the world of beauty and
clarity from which we evolved.

Castles and clouds, men and lives, all intertwined
into a miasma of experience, far too intricate to
ever sort into the firm acceptance of youth. We
must cast our convictions into the pit of past
experiences, and reach out anew, touch and taste
free of previous knowledge. To see a leaf once
again as a small piece of magic, to watch a
rainbow form itself in the rain-saturated sky, to
stop ... and take the time for living in the
Spring freshness of our days. This we must do.

Spring never passes from our lives. We are not
the seasons, evolving one into the other. We are
the totality of ourselves, carrying Spring with us
into the lands of Summer, Autumn and Winter. We
transport our innocence with our maturity into new
realms of experience. To leave innocence behind,
to stray from this most important attribute is to
kill an essential part of ourselves - our godhood.

Castles and clouds molded by hands of the eternally
young, given _life_ by the being of youth - found
within all of us ... This is our purpose, our goal
which we seek in nebulous dreams, hidden dis-satis-
factions, secret desires. We seek to bring this
forth, and in doing so, create our new and
wondrous reality of life everlasting.

***

How can you speak of loneliness
When the whole universe
Wheels within
                    and around
            you?

How can you think emptiness
When all that man is
                    and will be
            echoes within
The corridors of your heart?

How can you know loneliness
When but one thought away
Is the vast reality
                    of all times past
            and yet to be?

Other imagery books by David A Wilson

Alchemy of The Mind   (1969) $1.50
"Knowledge in dust, wisdom tattered and yellowed
by vengeful time ..." 22 poems, 40 pages.

Bits and Pieces   (1969) $1.50
A collection of short essays, pieces of thought,
bits of inspiration. 40 pages.

the Song of The Sea   (1970) $1.50
The epic poem is 320 lines, capturing the vast-
ness of the sea; 17 other poems, 40 pages.

Eternity Revisited   (1971) $2.00
Poetry, dimensionless in concept; limitless in
thought. The key motif is Depth. 48 pages.

Time: Sweet Bandit   (1974) $1.50
An interweaving of the enigma haunting everyone.
Featuring "Opus". Poetry & prose, 40 pages.

The Harvesting of America   (1976) $1.50
An epic poem. The future is locked in the seed
of our past, the seed of our future. 40 pages.

The Third World War   (1976) $1.00
A protest on the potent possibility ...
                              16 pages.

To order, enclose a check payable to Lorien House,
including $.60 postage and 4% sales tax if a NC
resident. Send to Lorien House, P.O. Box 1112,
Black Mountain, NC 28711